# Speech Practice

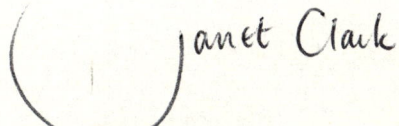

A C30 cassette is available which contains recording of possible interpretations of some of the exercises in *Speech Practice* and *Voice Production and Speech*. The recordings were made by the author of the two books, Greta Colson, with a group of her students at the New College of Speech and Drama, London, where she is Principal Lecturer.

## Speech Practice
Greta Colson

Side one covers some of the exercises in this book: 1, 8, 16, 23, 24, 34, 25, 42, 43, 48, 53, 82, 92, 135, 159.

## Voice Production and Speech
Greta Colson

Side two covers the additional exercises listed under the Appendix on page 81 of the book. The exercises demonstrated are: 3, 4, 5, 7, 8, 10, 11, 12 (two interpretations) and 13 (parts i, ii, iii, iv, v, vi).

# Speech Practice

*by*

## GRETA COLSON

*Principal Lecturer in charge of Voice, New College of Speech and Drama*

PITMAN

PITMAN PUBLISHING LIMITED
39 Parker Street, London WC2B 5PB

*Associated Companies*
Copp Clark Ltd, Toronto
Fearon Pitman Publishers Inc, San Francisco
Pitman Publishing New Zealand Ltd, Wellington
Pitman Publishing Pty Ltd, Melbourne

© Greta Colson, 1967, 1970, 1973

First published, 1967
Second edition, 1970
Third edition (under Pitman imprint), 1973
Reprinted 1975, 1978

Reproduced and printed by photolithography and bound in Great Britain
at The Pitman Press, Bath

ISBN 0 273 00046 2

# INTRODUCTION

When using the material making up this book it would help to bear in mind the following points—

1    They are intended as material to exercise the speech organs and re-educate them should speech habits be poor; also to increase awareness of sounds and words and the sensation of them in the mouth; so concentrate on dexterity of the speech organs.

2    Avoid warping your speech: keep it easy, natural and your own, but at the same time fully alive.

3    Be sensitive to speech tunes: your own are likely to be dictated by your regional environment. Avoid monotony in using these and keep your ears alert to other people's.

4    During this practice you are going to be aware of what you are doing with your voice and speech. Conscious use of them is confined to this preparatory period; the skill gained at this stage gives freedom from technical difficulties later. Section X is intended to bridge the gap between vocal practice and full interpretation; the thought content, mood and style of each passage should be carefully realized. The aim is to enable you to reach the difficult, demanding material in Section XI equipped with the ability to use language in exact sympathy

with your intentions. The degree of your success at this stage should be assessed by a listener; preferably by your teacher.

5     The nature of this collection has placed emphasis on interpretation. Parallel with this, and eventually out-stripping it, should be your own creative use of language.

GRETA COLSON

*For permission to reprint copyright matter the following acknowledgements are made—*

"King Charles the First" from *Kings and Other Things* by Hugh Chesterman, to the author and Messrs. Methuen & Co. Ltd.; extract from "Moon Man" by Fay Hampson, to the author; "ga boga libo," "bula bubulala," "pip pipio," "kah kah cacakjeda," "kokro co rico," "Loop," "Eastender, extender," "McAllister" and a stanza from "Chamber Music" by Bob Cobbing to the author; "Three Sundays and a Summary" by Liz Holmes, to the author; *The Complete Poems of Gerard Manley Hopkins*, to the Oxford University Press; "The Horses" from *The Hawk in the Rain* and "Music on the Moon" from *The Earth-Owl and Other Moon People* by Ted Hughes, to the author and Messrs. Faber and Faber Ltd.; "Cider with Rosie" by Laurie Lee, to the author and The Hogarth Press Ltd.; "The Edge of Day" from *My Many-Coated Man* by Laurie Lee, to the author and Messrs. André Deutsch Ltd.; "Off the Ground" by Walter de la Mare, to the Literary Trustees of Walter de la Mare and the Society of Authors; "The Tickle Rhyme" by Ian Serraillier to the author and to the Oxford University Press, in whose book *The Tale of the Monster Horse* it appeared; "Trio for Two Cats and a Trombone" from *Façade and Other Poems 1920-35* by Edith Sitwell, to Messrs. Gerald Duckworth & Co. Ltd.; extract from *Be Good, Sweet Maid* by C. E. Webber to the author.

# SECTIONS

If voice and speech are to be vital and flexible, muscles must be trained; Sections 1 and 2 deal specifically with this.

Dexterity is increased by—

and by—

Sometimes the rhythm of our speech echoes meaning and strengthens it. Verse affords easy practice for this; several of the following examples may make you want to move as well as speak.

The following Section makes varying demands on the resonance of the voice—

Pitch is exercised by—

More subtle demands on pitch are made by pointing—

The odds and ends are gathered up into—

Vocal sensitivity is further exercised by—

Finally come considerable hurdles in—

# One

# LIP EXAMPLES

*In some sound patterns the lips have special importance.*

**1** *Pimlico, Pamlico, Pumpkin and peas,*
*Pepper them properly else you will sneeze:*
*Pop in a pipkin and leave them till one,*
*Pimlico, Pamlico, then they'll be done.*

   (*Nursery rhyme*)

**2** *When the pods went pop on the broom, green*
   *broom*
*And apples began to be golden-skinn'd,*
*We harbour'd a stag in the Priory coomb,*
*And we feather'd his trail up-wind, up-wind,*
*We feather'd his trail up-wind.*

   (*John Davidson, "A Runnable Stag"*)

**3** *The moan of doves in immemorial elms,*
*And murmuring of innumerable bees.*

   (*Tennyson, "Come Down, O Maid"*)

**4** ga                                          (*il s*)
boga libo
bagi loba
bigo labi
obo aga ili bo
ba igi olo aba
ibi ogo ala bi
bo bo gali
ba lo giba
bi bi gola
o baga ili bo
ba igi o loba
i bogo ala bi
gali bobo gali
ba lo giba giba
go la bibi go la
bobo gali gali bobo
baba ligi gola baba
bibi lago lago bibi
gaga lili bobo gaga
gigi balo balo gigi
gogo bali bali gogo
boga libo libo gali
bagi balo logi balo
bigo labi bigo labi
boga libo bo aga ili obo
bagi loba aba igi olo ba
bigo labi bi ogo ala ibi
bo bo gali aga ili bo
ba lo giba a bigi o loba
bi bi gola bi ogo ala bi


go ba bi lo ga ba bi la gi bo ba li bo
(*For two or more voices in counterpoint*)

o

gali bobo gali bobo aga ili bobo
balo giba giba baba igi olo baba
gola bibi gola bibi ogo ala bibi
ga li bobo gali gaga bobo ili gaga
ba lo giba giba gigi baba olo gigi
go la bibi gola gogo bibi ala gogo
bo gali bo bo gali gaga lili bobo gaga
ba giba lo lo giba gigi balo balo gigi
bi gola bi bi gola gogo bali bali gogo
boga libo libo gali libo gali gali lobo
bagi balo logi balo logi balo balo loga
bigo labi bigo labi labi bigo labi bogo
gogo ala bibi gogo bibi ala ogo bibi
gigi olo baba gigi baba olo igi baba
gaga ili bobo gaga bobo ili aga bobo
a labi i bogo gola bibi
o loba ba igi giba balo
i libo o baga gali bobo
ili ogo ala ibi bi ala ogo ibi
ba olo igi aba aba olo igi ba
obo ili aga bo bo aga ili bo
bigo labi
bagi loba
boga libo
bo li
ga bo
ba lo
gi ba
bo
ga
li
ga bi lo ba gi bo la bi go ba li
  bo                          (*Bob Cobbing*)

5 *Willows whiten, aspens quiver,*
*Little breezes dusk and shiver*
*Thro' the wave that runs for ever*
*By the island in the river*
*Flowing down to Camelot.*

(*Tennyson, "The Lady of Shalott"*)

6 *The gloom of the sea,*
*The gloom of the sky,*
*Hung brooding over all;*
*The seagulls knew*
*And landwards flew*
*Swooping with muted call.*

7 *bubla bubulala*
*bamberoo bumbharali*
*bomboolios bumberooli*
*tse tse ntsintsi*
*bumberoo bambharali*
*bumboolios bamberooli*
*tse tse ntsintsi*
*booboo bumrali*
*bubuluza boozuza*
*bomboloza zezu*

(*Bob Cobbing*)

8 *pip*
*pipio pigione*
*pippione piccione pipare*
*pinire pipiare pigiolare pippionare*
*pippolini pipelni pipegni*
*pipay pipok*
*pip*

(*Bob Cobbing*)

*Two*

# TONGUE EXAMPLES

*In some sound patterns the tongue has special impor-*
*tance.*

**9** *To sit in solemn silence in a dull, dark dock*
*In a pestilential prison, with a life-long lock.*
*Awaiting the sensation of a short, sharp shock,*
*From a cheap and chippy chopper on a big black*
*block!*       (**W. S. Gilbert**)

**10** *The splendour falls on castle walls*
*And snowy summits old in story:*
*The long light shakes across the lakes,*
*And the wild cataract leaps in glory.*
    *(Tennyson, "The Splendour Falls")*

**11** *You spotted snakes with double tongue,*
*Thorny hedgehogs, be not seen;*
*Newts and blind-worms, do no wrong;*
*Come not near our fairy queen.*

*Philomel, with melody,*
*Sing in our sweet lullaby;*
*Lulla, lulla, lullaby; lulla, lulla, lullaby.*
*(Shakespeare, "A Midsummer Night's*
                          *Dream")*

**12** *And on the tawny sands and shelves,*
*Trip the pert fairies and the dapper elves;*
*By dimpled brook and fountain brim,*
*The wood-nymphs, decked with daisies trim,*
*Their merry wakes and pastimes keep.*
                              (*Milton, "Comus"*)

**13** *Toe, trip and go,*
*Heel, tread a bank,*
*Shin, shinny shank,*
*Knee, knick a knack,*
*Thigh, thick a thack,*
*Leg, lope along,*
*Lean and strong.*
          (*Nursery rhyme*)

**14** *A trot and a canter, a gallop and over,*
*Out of the saddle and roll in the clover.*
                              (*Nursery rhyme*)

**15** *A dis, a dos, a green grass,*
*A dis, a doh, a dare,*
*Come and join our deft dance,*
*Join it, pair by pair.*
          (*Nursery rhyme*)

**16** *timpa tampa*              *twonk*
*tump tup*                *rol rol rol*
*tumbuk timno*            *twonk twonk*
*tumbak tamno*            *rol rol rol rol*
*timpa tampa*             *twonk*
*tomp tump*               *rol rol rol rol rol*
*tom tom tump tup*        *twonk twonk*
*tum tum tomp tump*       *rol rol rol rol rol rol*
                              (*Bob Cobbing*)

**17** *But Kate, the prettiest Kate in Christendom;*
*Kate of Kate-Hall, my super-dainty Kate.*
(*Shakespeare, "The Taming of the Shrew"*)

**18** *While the cock with lively din,*
*Scatters the rear of darkness thin,*
*And to the stack or the barn-door,*
*Stoutly struts his dames before.*
(*Milton, "L'Allegro"*)

**19** *Three jolly Farmers*
*Once bet a pound*
*Each dance the others would*
*Off the ground.*
*Out of their coats*
*They slipped right soon,*
*And neat and nicesome,*
*Put each his shoon.*
*One—Two—Three!—*
*And away they go,*
*Not too fast,*
*And not too slow;*
*Out of the elm-tree's*
*Noonday shadow,*
*Into the sun*
*And across the meadow.*
*Past the schoolroom,*
*With knees well bent*
*Fingers a-flicking,*
*They dancing went.*
*Up sides and over,*
*And round and round,*
*They crossed click-clacking,*

*The Parish bound.*
*By Tupman's meadow*
*They did their mile,*
*Tee-to-tum*
*On a three-barred stile.*
*Then straight through Whipham,*
*Downhill to Week,*
*Footing it lightsome,*
*But not too quick,*
*Up fields to Watchet,*
*And on through Wye,*
*Till seven fine churches*
*They'd seen skip by—*
*Seven fine churches,*
*And five old mills,*
*Farms in the valley,*
*And sheep on the hills;*
*Withy—Wellover—*
*Wassop—Wo—*
*Like an old clock*
*Their heels did go.*
*A league and a league*
*And a league they went,*
*And not one weary,*
*And not one spent.*
*And lo, and behold!*
*Past Willow-cum-Leigh*
*Stretched with its waters*
*The great green sea.*

*(Walter de la Mare,*
                 *"Off the Ground")*

*Three*

# TWISTERS

*Test your muscular dexterity with these twisters!*

**20** Both bustled busily buttering buns.

**21** Betty Botter bought some butter,
But, she said, the butter's bitter;
If I put it in my batter
It will make my batter bitter.
So she bought a bit of butter
Better than her bitter butter,
And she put it in her batter,
And so the batter wasn't bitter.

(Traditional)

**22** Lots of hot coffee in a proper copper coffee-pot.

(Traditional)

**23** Crispy, crunchy, crinkly crackling.

**24** A dozen double adapters. (*3 times*)

**25** Who are you sir, tell me who?
What's that to you, sir? Who, sir? You, sir?
What's that to who, sir? Who, sir? You!

(Traditional)

**26** *Great galumphing globes of gas.*
*(Lewis Carroll)*

**27** *Peter Piper picked a peck of pickled pepper;*
*A peck of pickled pepper Peter Piper picked.*
*If Peter Piper picked a peck of pickled pepper,*
*Where's the peck of pickled pepper Peter Piper*
    *picked?*
*(Traditional)*

**28** *And I'm a peppery kind of King,*
*Who's indisposed to parleying;*
*To fit my wit to a bit or a chit,*
*And that's the long and the short of it!*
*(W. S. Gilbert)*

**29** *A hasp, a staple and a padlock. (3 times)*

**30** *A pinch of paprika pepper popped in a paper*
    *poke.*
*(Traditional)*

**31** *Pride, prejudice, prunes and prisms.* (3 times)

**32** *Round and round the rugged rocks*
*The ragged rascals ran their rural races.*
*(Traditional)*

**33** *Robert Rowley rolled a round roll round,*
*A round roll Robert Rowley rolled round;*
*Where rolled the round roll Robert Rowley*
    *rolled round?*
*(Nursery rhyme)*

**34** *Succulent steaks and sizzling sausages.* (3 times)

**35** *Silky soapsuds sparkling in the sun.* (3 times)

**36** *Theophilus Thistlewaite,*
*The unsuccessful thistle-sifter,*
*Thrust three thousand thistles*
*Through the thick of his thumb*
*When sifting a sieve of unsifted thistles.*
                    *(Traditional)*

**37** *Two toads totally tired of trying to trot to*
    *Tetbury.*
                    *(Traditional)*

**38** *International intermonetary fund.* (3 times)

**39** *Interplanetary auditory discrimination.* (3 times)

**40** *You can take a tub with a rub and a scrub in a*
    *two-foot tank of tin,*
*You can stand and look at the whirling brook*
    *and think about jumping in,*
*You can chatter and shake in the cold black*
    *lake, but the kind of bath for me,*
*Is to take a dip from the side of a ship, in the*
    *trough of the rolling sea.*
                    *(W. S. Gilbert)*

**41** *Sixty-six distinguished bespectacled boffins.* (3
    times)

**42** *kah kah cacakjeda*
*kra kra grika*
*kra kra kra kacha*
*kah chacha kah graji*
*khrij khrij*
*kra grika gra chacha*
*khrij karat khrij karot*
*gra graji grika chacha*
*kra klah kah*

(*Bob Cobbing*)

*Four*

# SPEED EXAMPLES

*A quick rate, or the illusion of it, is demanded by—*

**43**  *A centipede was happy quite,*
*Until the toad in fun*
*Said, "Pray which leg goes after which?"*
*Which worked her mind to such a pitch*
*She lay distracted in the ditch*
*Considering how to run.*

> (*Mrs. Edward Craster, "An Animal*
> *Anthology"*)

**44**  *Boot, saddle, to horse and away!*
*Rescue my castle before the hot day*
*Brightens to blue from its silvery grey,*
*Boot, saddle, to horse, and away!*
*Ride past the suburbs, asleep as you'd say;*
*Many's the friend there, will listen and pray*
*"God's luck to gallants that strike up the lay—*
*Boot, saddle, to horse, and away!"*

> (*Browning, "Boot and Saddle"*)

**45**  *Chop, chop, choppity chop:*
*Chop off the bottom and chop off the top:*
*What we have left we will pop in the pot,*
*Chop, chop, choppity chop.*

**46** *I am the very model of a modern Major-General,*
*I've information vegetable, animal and mineral,*
*I know the kings of England, and I quote the fights historical,*
*From Marathon to Waterloo, in order categorical.*

*I'm very well acquainted too with matters mathematical,*
*I understand equations, both the simple and quadratical,*
*About binomial theorem I'm teeming with a lot o' news—*
*With many cheerful facts about the square of the hypotenuse.*

*I'm very good at integral and differential calculus,*
*I know the scientific names of beings animalculous;*
*In short, in matters vegetable, animal and mineral,*
*I am the very model of a modern Major-General.*
*(W. S. Gilbert)*

**47** *Here's a first-rate opportunity*
*To get married with impunity,*
*To indulge in the felicity*
*Of unbounded domesticity.*
*You shall quickly be personified,*
*Conjugally matrimonified,*
*By a doctor of divinity,*
*Who resides in this vicinity.*
*(W. S. Gilbert)*

**48** *McAllister*
*Macalpine*
*Macarthur*
*Macaulay*
*Macbean*
*MacBrayne*
*MacBryde*
*MacCallum*
*McCarthy*
*McCleary*
*McCormack*
*McCulloch*
*McElroy*
*MacEwan*
*McGhee*
*McGill*
*McGowan*
*McGrath*

*MacGregor*
*McGuiness*
*MacGuire*
*McKay*
*McKellar*
*McKenna*
*McKlean*
*McLellan*
*McLennan*
*MacLeod*
*Macnamara*
*Macnaughton*
*MacPherson*
*McQueen*
*McSorley*
*McSweeney*
*McTaggart*

(*Bob Cobbing*)

**49** *In enterprise of martial kind,*
*When there was any fighting,*
*He led his regiment from behind—*
*He found it less exciting.*
*But when away his regiment ran,*
*His place was at the fore, O—*
*That celebrated,*
*Cultivated,*
*Underrated*
*Nobleman,*
*The Duke of Plaza-Toro!*

(*W. S. Gilbert*)

**50** *kokro co rico*
*koklo quiquiriqui*
*okoko okoka*
*kuku kukkata*
*kukko caracaca*
*kukuk kaluruk*
*kukuduna kukukasi*
*kokro coquelicot*
*koklo tsu koklo no*
    *(Bob Cobbing)*


**51** *When you're lying awake with a dismal head-ache, and repose is taboo'd by anxiety,*

*I conceive you may use any language you choose to indulge in, without impropriety;*

*For your brain is on fire—the bedclothes conspire of usual slumber to plunder you:*

*First your counterpane goes, and uncovers your toes, and your sheet slips demurely from under you;*

*Then the blanketing tickles—you feel like mixed pickles so terribly sharp is the pricking.*

*And you're hot, and you're cross, and you tumble and toss till there's nothing 'twixt you and the ticking.*

*Then the bedclothes all creep to the ground in a heap, and you pick 'em up all in a tangle;*

*Next your pillow resigns and politely declines to remain at its usual angle!*

*Well, you get some repose in the form of a doze, with hot eyeballs and head ever aching,*

*But your slumbering teems with such horrible dreams that you'd very much better be waking;*

*For you dream you are crossing the Channel, and tossing about in a steamer from Harwich—*

*Which is something between a large bathing-machine and a very small second-class carriage;*

*And bound on that journey you find your attorney (who started that morning from Devon);*

*He's a bit undersized, and you don't feel surprised when he tells you he's only eleven.*

*And he and the crew are on bicycles too—which they've somehow or other invested in—*

*And he's telling the tars all the particulars of a company he's interested in—*

*It's a scheme of devices, to get at low prices, all goods from cough mixtures to cables*

*(Which tickled the sailors), by treating retailers as though they were all vegetables—*

*The shares are a penny, and ever so many are taken by Rothschild and Baring,*

*And just as a few are allotted to you, you awake with a shudder despairing—*

*You're a regular wreck, with a crick in your neck, and no wonder you snore, for your head's on the floor, and you've needles and pins from your soles to your shins, and your flesh is a-creep, for your left leg's asleep, and you've cramp in your toes, and a fly on your nose, and some fluff in your lung, and a feverish tongue, and a thirst that's intense, and a*

general sense that you haven't been sleeping
in clover;
But the darkness has passed, and it's daylight
at last, and the night has been long—ditto,
ditto my song—and thank goodness they're
both of them over!

(*W. S. Gilbert*)


**52** I sprang to the stirrup, and Joris, and he;
I galloped, Dirck galloped, we galloped all three;
"Good speed!" cried the watch, as the gate-
bolts undrew;
"Speed!" echoed the wall to us galloping
through;
Behind shut the postern, the lights sank to rest,
And into the midnight we galloped abreast.


Not a word to each other; we kept the great pace
Neck by neck, stride by stride, never changing
our place;
I turned in my saddle and made its girth tight,
Then shortened each stirrup, and set the pique
right,
Rebuckled the cheek-strap, chained slacker the
bit,
Nor galloped less steadily Roland a whit.


Then I cast loose my buffcoat, each holster let
fall,
Shook off both my jack-boots, let go belt and all,
Stood up in the stirrup, leaned, patted his ear,
Called my Roland his pet-name, my horse with-
out peer;

*Clapped my hands, laughed and sang, any noise,*
  *bad or good,*
*Till at length into Aix Roland galloped and*
  *stood.*

*(Browning, "How They Brought the*
  *Good News from Ghent to Aix")*

# Five

# RHYTHM EXAMPLES

**53** *There once was a man who could execute*
*Old Zip Coon on a yellow flute,*
*And many another tune to boot,*
*But he couldn't make a penny*
*With his tootletitoot.*
*Tootle ootle ootle, tootle-ti-toot.*

*One day he met with a singular*
*Quaint old man with a big tuba,*
*Who said he'd travelled wide and far,*
*But he couldn't make a penny*
*With his oompapa.*
*Oompa, oompa, oompapa,*
*Tootle ootle ootle oompapa.*

*They met two men who were travelling*
*With a big bass drum and a cymbal thing,*
*Who said they'd banged since early spring*
*But they couldn't make a penny*
*With their boom zingzing.*
*Boom zing, boom zing, boom zing zing,*
*Tootle ootle oompa*
*Boom zing zing.*

*So*
*The man with the flute went tootle-ti-toot,*

*And the other man he went oompa,*
*And the men with the drum and the cymbal thing*
*Went boom, boom, boom boom boom, zing*
   *zing.*
*And, oh, the pennies that the people fling*
*When they hear that tootle oompa boom zing*
   *zing!*
*Boom zing, boom zing, boom zing zing,*
*Tootle ootle oompa boom zing zing.*

                     (*Traditional*

**54** *Bang, bang, bang goes the drum,*
*Boom, boom, the soldiers come.*

           (*Nursery rhyme*)

**55** *The double double double beat*
*Of the thundering drum*
*Cries "Hark! the foes come!*
*Charge! Charge! 'Tis too late to retreat!"*

     (*Dryden, "Song for St. Cecilia's Day"*)

**56** *Though in body and in mind,*
*Tarantará, tarantará!*
*We are timidly inclined,*
*Tarantará!*
*And anything but blind,*
*Tarantará, tarantará!*
*To the danger that's behind,*
*Tarantará!*
*Yet, when the danger's near,*
*Tarántará, tarántará!*
*We manage to appear,*
*Tarantará!*

*As insensible to fear*
*As anybody here,*
*Tarántará, tarantará-rá-rá-rá-rá!*

(*W. S. Gilbert*)


**57** *Kentish Sir Byng stood for his King,*
*Bidding the crop-headed Parliament swing:*
*And pressing a troop unable to stoop,*
*And see the rogues flourish and honest folk*
   *droop,*
*Marched them along, fifty-score strong,*
*Great-hearted gentlemen, singing this song.*

*God for King Charles! Pym and such carles*
*To the Devil that prompts 'em their treasonous*
   *parles!*
*Cavaliers, up! Lips from the cup,*
*Hands from the pasty, nor bite take nor sup*
*Till you're marching along, fifty-score strong,*
*Great-hearted gentlemen singing this song.*

(*Browning, "Marching Song"*)


**58** *Over the hills and o'er the main,*
*To Flanders, Portugal or Spain:*
*The queen commands, and we'll obey—*
*Over the hills and far away.*

(*Song—pre-1700*)


**59** *For there in front of the men were marching*
*With feet that made no mark,*
*The grey old ghosts of the ancient fighters*
*Come back again from the dark.*

**60** *East-ender extender East India hinderer*
*East wind be twinned he syndicate sanity*
*Twixt and betweenity first name first dame*
*furtive*
*Flirtatious Eurasian Asian Beudantite bevel*
*Bigeminal seminal betulin betterment*
*Betumbled lumbered cumbered custard*
*Crisis cripple criss-cross cribble*
*Cranium crinoid crinkle crankle*
*Crinkum chasm cataclasm*
*Cataclysm biblioclasm*
*Biblioclast biblioklept*
*Bibliokleptomania*
*Bibliophagic bibliophagist*
*Bibliopegistical*
*Bibliomanic bibliomaniac*
*Bibble*
    *babble*
      *bibitory*
*Bigeminal seminal Betjeman bafflement*
*East-ender extender East India hinderer*
*East wind be twinned syndicate sanity*
*Flirtatious Eurasian Asian Beudantite level*
*The devil*

                (*Bob Cobbing*)

**61** *Hark, hark, the dogs do bark,*
*The beggars are coming to town;*
*Some in jags, some in rags,*
*And some in velvet gowns.*

          (*Nursery rhyme*)

**62** *Sometimes a troop of damsels glad,*
*An Abbot on an ambling pad,*
*Sometimes a curly shepherd lad,*
*Or long-hair'd page in crimson clad*
*Goes by to tower'd Camelot.*

(*Tennyson, "The Lady of Shalott"*)

**63** *Hey diddle dinkety, poppety, pet,*
*The merchants of London they wear scarlet;*
*Silk in the collar and gold in the hem,*
*So merrily march the merchant men.*

(*Nursery rhyme*)

**64** *One, two, three, four, five, six, seven,*
*All good children go to heaven.*

(*Nursery rhyme*)

**65** *One, two, buckle my shoe;*
*Three, four, knock at the door;*
*Five, six, pick up sticks;*
*Seven, eight, lay them straight;*
*Nine, ten, a big fat hen;*
*Eleven, twelve, dig and delve;*
*Thirteen, fourteen, maids a-courting;*
*Fifteen, sixteen, maids in the kitchen;*
*Seventeen, eighteen, maids in waiting;*
*Nineteen, twenty, my plate's empty.*

(*Nursery rhyme*)

**66** *King and Queen of the Pelicans we;*
*No other birds so grand we see!*
*None but we have feet like fins!*
*With lovely leathery throats and chins!*

*Ploffskin, pluffskin, Pelican jee!*
*We think no birds as happy as we!*
*Plumpskin, Ploshkin, Pelican Jill!*
*We think so then, and we thought so still!*
  (*Edward Lear, "The Pelican Chorus"*)


**67** *You should*
        *See me dance the polka,*
        *As over the ground I fly;*
        *You should see me dance the polka*
        *As all the world whirls by.*
            *Tra la la la lá laa*
            *Tra la la la lá laa*
            *Tra la la la lá laa*
            *LAA!*


**68** *Here we come loopy loo,*
*Here we come loopy lay,*
*Here we come loopy loo,*
*All in a morning in May.*
        (*Nursery rhyme*)


**69** *A carrion crow sat on an oak,*
        *Fol de riddle, lol de riddle, hi ding do,*
*Watching a tailor shape his cloak;*
        *Sing heigh ho, the carrion crow,*
        *Fol de riddle, lol de riddle, hi ding do.*

*Wife, bring me my old bent bow,*
        *Fol de riddle, lol de riddle, high ding do.*
*That I may shoot yon carrion crow,*
        *Sing heigh ho, the carrion crow,*
        *Fol de riddle, lol de riddle, hi ding do.*

*The tailor he shot, and missed his mark,*
  *Fol de riddle, lol de riddle, hi ding do.*
*And shot his own sow right through the heart,*
  *Sing heigh ho the carrion crow,*
  *Fol de riddle, lol de riddle, hi ding do.*

*Wife, bring brandy in a spoon,*
  *Fol de riddle, lol de riddle, high ding do,*
*For our old sow is in a swoon;*
  *Sing heigh ho the carrion crow,*
  *Fol de riddle, lol de riddle, high ding do.*
                              (*Traditional*)

**70** *There was an old woman who rode on a broom,*
    *With a high gee go, gee humble;*
    *And she took her old cat behind for a groom,*
    *With a bimble, bamble, bumble.*
                              (*Nursery rhyme*)

**71** *For a charm of powerful trouble,*
    *Like a hell-broth boil and bubble,*
    *Double, double toil and trouble;*
    *Fire burn and cauldron bubble.*
          (*Shakespeare, "Macbeth"*)

**72** *Fee, fie, foh, fum,*
    *I smell the blood of an Englishman.*
    *Be he alive or be he dead*
    *I'll grind his bones to make my bread.*
                              (*Traditional*)

**73** *I have seen old ships sail like swans asleep*
    *Beyond the village that men still call Tyre,*

*With leaden age o'ercargoed, dipping deep*
*For Famagusta and the hidden sun*
*That rings black Cyprus with a lake of fire;*
*And all those ships were certainly so old*
*Who knows how oft with squat and noisy gun,*
*Questing brown slaves or Syrian oranges,*
*The pirate Genoese*
*Hell-raked them till they rolled*
*Blood, water, fruit and corpses up the hold.*
*But now through friendly seas they softly run,*
*Painted the mid-sea blue or shore-sea green,*
*Still patterned with the vine and grapes in gold.*

       (*James Elroy Flecker, "The Old Ships"*)

**74** *I chatter over stony ways,*
*In little sharps and trebles,*
*I bubble into eddying bays,*
*I babble on the pebbles.*

   (*Tennyson, "The Brook"*)

**75** *Coffee*
*Coffee*
*Cheese and biscuits*
*Cheese and biscuits*
*Ginger pudding and cream*
*Ginger pudding and cream*
*Boiled beef and pease-pudding*
*Boiled beef and pease-pudding*
*Fish and chips*
*Fish and chips*
*Fish and chips*
*Fish and chips*
*Soup*
*SOU . . . P*       (*Train rhythm—traditional*)

**76** *Over the sea our galleys went,*
*With cleaving prows in order brave*
*To a speeding wind and a bounding wave—*
*A gallant armament.*

> (*Browning, "The Wanderers"*)

**77** I like to watch an old boatman rowing, especially one who has been hired by the hour. There is something so beautifully calm and restful about his method. It is so free from that fretful haste, that vehement striving, that is every day becoming more and more the bane of nineteenth-century life. He is not for ever straining himself to pass all the other boats. If another boat overtakes him it does not annoy him; as a matter of fact, they do all overtake him and pass him—all those that are going his way. This would trouble and irritate some people; the sublime equanimity of the hired boatman under the ordeal affords us a beautiful lesson against ambition and uppishness.

> (*Jerome K. Jerome, "Three Men in a Boat"*)

**78** *There's a Black Ball barque coming down the*
    *river,*
*Blow, bullies, blow;*
*There's a Black Ball barque coming down the*
    *river,*
*Blow, my bully boys, blow.*

*You'll brighten brass, and you'll scrape the
   cable,*
*Blow bullies, blow;*
*You'll brighten brass, and you'll scrape the
   cable,*
*Blow, my bully boys, blow.*

(*Traditional*)

*Six*

# *TONE EXAMPLES*

*These passages are brought alive mainly by the general quality of the voice.*

**79** *The Lotos blooms below the barren peak;*
*The Lotos blows by every winding creek;*
*All day the wind breathes low with mellower*
*tone.*

> *(Tennyson, "The Lotos-Eaters")*

**80** *When the hounds of spring are on winter's*
*traces,*
*The mother of months in meadow and plain*
*Fills the shadows and windy places*
*With lisp of leaves and ripple of rain.*

> *(Swinburne, "Atalanta Alergon")*

**81** *Therefore awake, make haste I say,*
*And let us without staying,*
*All in our gowns of green so gay,*
*Into the park a-maying.*

*(17th century)*


**82** *Loop*
*La lune Loop*
*Ontala ontala tala tala*
*Low loom Bleep*
*Bleep la lune Loop*
*La nuit est morte*

*Bleep*
*La lune Loop*
*Le jour est mort*
*Ontala tala tala*

*La loupe . . .*
*Tala tala*
*Les runes Droop*
*Langage*
*Est mort*

*(Bob Cobbing)*


**83** *The trumpet's loud clangour*
*Excites us to arms,*
*With shrill notes of anger,*
*And mortal alarms.*

*(Dryden, "Song for*
*St. Cecilia's Day")*

**84** *When the night wind howls in the chimney cowls,*
*    and the bat in the moonlight flies,*
*And inky clouds, like funeral shrouds, sail over*
*    the midnight skies—*
*When the footpads quail at the night-bird's wail,*
*    the black dogs bay at the moon,*
*Then is the spectres' holiday—then is the ghosts'*
*    high-noon!*

*(W. S. Gilbert)*

**85** *Lead out the pageant: sad and slow,*
*As fits an universal woe,*
*Let the long, long procession go,*
*And let the sorrowing crowd about it grow,*
*And let the mournful martial music blow;*
*The last great Englishman is low.*

*(Tennyson, "Ode on the Death of the*
*Duke of Wellington")*

**86** *But as they left the dark'ning heath,*
*More desperate grew the strife of death.*
*The English shafts in volleys hail'd,*
*In headlong charge their horse assail'd;*
*Front, flank, and rear, the squadrons sweep*
*To break the Scottish circle deep,*
*That fought around their king.*

*(Sir Walter Scott)*

**87** *There is sweet music here that softer falls*
*Than petals from blown roses on the grass,*
*Or night-dews on still waters between walls*
*Of shadowy granite, in a gleaming pass;*

*Music that gentlier on the spirit lies,*
*Than tir'd eyelids upon tir'd eyes;*
*Music that brings sweet sleep down from the*
  *blissful skies.*
*Here are cool mosses deep,*
*And thro' the moss the ivies creep,*
*And in the stream the long-leaved flowers weep,*
*And from the craggy ledge the poppy hangs in*
  *sleep.*

                    *(Tennyson, "The Lotos-Eaters")*


**88** *The moanings of the homeless sea,*
   *The sound of streams that swift or slow*
   *Draw down Aeonian hill, and sow*
   *The dust of continents to be.*

              *(Tennyson, "In Memoriam")*


**89** *Come unto these yellow sands,*
   *And there take hands:*
   *Curtsied when you have, and kiss'd—*
   *The wild waves whist—*
   *Foot it featly here and there;*
   *Hark, hark!*
   *The watch-dogs bark;*
   *Hark, hark! I hear*
   *The strain of strutting Chanticleer*
        *Cock-a-diddle-dow.*

              *(Shakespeare, "Song")*


**90** *Clear and cool*
   *Clear and cool*
   *By laughing shallow and dreaming pool.*

*Cool and clear*
*Cool and clear*
*By shining shingle and foaming weir.*
> (*Tennyson, "The Brook"*)

**91** *So Goodluck came, and on my roof did light,*
*Like noiseless snow; or as the dew of night:*
*Not all at once, but gently, as the trees*
*Are, by the sunbeams, tickled by degrees.*

**92** *Lo! in the middle of the wood*
*The folded leaf is woo'd from out the bud*
*With winds upon the branch, and there*
*Grows green and broad and takes no care,*
*Sun-steep'd at noon, and in the moon*
*Nightly dew-fed; and turning yellow*
*Falls, and floats adown the air.*
> (*Tennyson, "The Lotos-Eaters"*)

**93** *Tis a dull sight*
*To see the year dying,*
*When winter winds*
*Set the yellow woods sighing:*
*Sighing, O sighing.*
> (*Edward Fitzgerald, "Old Song"*)

**94** *O hark, O hear! how thin and clear,*
*And thinner, clearer, farther going!*
*O sweet and far from cliff and scar*
*The horns of Elfland faintly blowing!*
*Blow let us hear the purple glens replying;*
*Blow, bugle; answer, echoes, dying, dying, dying.*
> (*Tennyson, "The Splendour Falls"*)

**95** *And slowly slowly more and more,*
*The moony vapour rolling round the King,*
*Who seemed the phantom of a giant in it,*
*Enwound him fold by fold,*
*And made him grey and greyer,*
*Till himself became as mist before her,*
*Moving ghost-like to his doom.*

> (*Tennyson, "Idylls of the King"*)

**96** *Sharp violins proclaim*
*Their jealous pangs and desperation,*
*Fury, frantic indignation,*
*Depth of pain, and height of passion*
*For the fair disdainful dame.*

> (*Dryden, "Song for St. Cecilia's*
> *Day"*)

# Seven

# *SONGS*

*You can speak or sing these examples. Try speaking them as rounds (line by line).*

**97** *How sweet the sound of chiming bells.*
   *(Sing this and make it sound like a peal of bells)*

**98** *I have a song to sing, O!*
   *Sing me your song, O!*
   *It is sung to the knell*
   *Of a churchyard bell,*
   *And a doleful dirge, ding dong, O!*

   *(W. S. Gilbert)*

**99** *Full fathom five thy father lies,*
   *Of his bones are coral made;*
   *Those are pearls that were his eyes:*
   *Nothing of him that doth fade,*
   *But doth suffer a sea-change*
   *Into something rich and strange.*
   *Sea-nymphs hourly ring his knell:*
   *Hark! now I hear them—*
      *Ding, dong, bell.*

   *(Shakespeare, "The Tempest")*

**100** *Or, to get merry,*
   *We sing some old rhyme*

*That made the wood ring again*
*In summer time—*
*Sweet summer time.*

(*Old song*)

**101** *My love sent me a chicken without a bone;*
*He sent me a cherry without a stone;*
*He sent me a book that no man could read;*
*He sent me a blanket without a thread.*

*How can there be a chicken without a bone?*
*How can there be a cherry without a stone?*
*How can there be a book that no man can read?*
*How can there be a blanket without a thread?*

*When the chicken's in the eggshell, there is no*
  *bone;*
*When the cherry's in the blossom, there is no*
  *stone;*
*When the book's in the press, no man can it*
  *read;*
*When the wool is on the sheep's back, there is no*
  *thread.*

(*Traditional*)

**102** *Here we go round the sun,*
*Here we go round the moon,*
*Here we go round the chimney-pots*
*On a Saturday afternoon.*

(*Nursery rhyme*)

**103** *Girls and boys come out to play,*
*The moon doth shine as bright as day;*

*Leave your supper and leave your sleep,*
*And come with your playfellows into the street.*

(*Nursery rhyme*)

**104** *Skip, skip, skip to my loo,*
*Skip, skip, skip to my loo,*
*Skip to my loo, my darling.*

(*Nursery rhyme*)

**105** *There was an old man named Michael Finnigan,*
*He grew whiskers on his chinigan,*
*The wind came out and blew them in agen,*
*Poor old Michael Finnigan—begin agen.*

(*Traditional*)

**106** *John Cook he had a little grey mare;*
        *Hee, haw, hum;*
*Her back stood up, and her bones they were*
    *bare;*
        *Hee, haw, hum.*

*John Cook was riding up Shooter's bank;*
        *Hee, haw, hum;*
*And there his nag did kick and prank;*
        *Hee, haw, hum.*

*John Cook was riding up Shooter's hill;*
        *Hee, haw, hum;*
*His mare fell down, and she made her will;*
        *Hee, haw, hum.*

The bridle and saddle were laid on the shelf;
   Hee, haw, hum;
If you want any more, you may sing it yourself;
   Hee, haw, hum.

                (*Traditional*)

**107**  Bobby Shaftoe's gone to sea,
Silver buckles at his knee;
He'll come back and marry me,
Bonny Bobby Shaftoe.

Bobby Shaftoe's tall and slim,
He's always dressed so neat and trim,
The ladies they all keek at him,
Bonny Bobby Shaftoe.

                (*Traditional*)

**108**  Lavender's blue, diddle, diddle,
Lavender's green;
When I am king, diddle, diddle,
You shall be queen.

Roses are red, diddle, diddle,
Violets are blue;
Because you love me, diddle, diddle,
I will love you.

                (*Traditional*)

**109**  White sands and grey sands,
Who'll buy my white sand?
Who'll buy my grey sand?       (Round)

      (*Traditional*)

**110** *London's burning! London's burning!*
*Fetch the engines! Fetch the engines!*
*Fire, fire! Fire, fire!*
*Pour on water! Pour on water!*

*(Traditional)*

# Eight

# RHYMES AND RIDDLES

*Rhymes and Riddles need point and innuendo.*

**111** *Liza, Elizabeth, Betsy and Bess,*
*They went to the woods to find a bird's nest;*
*They found a nest with four eggs in it,*
*They took one apiece and left three in it.*

(*Traditional*)

**112** *"Who's that tickling my back?" said the wall,*
*"Me," said a small*
*Caterpillar. "I'm learning*
*To crawl."*

(*Ian Serraillier, "The Tickle Rhyme"*)

**113** *There once were two cats of Kilkenny,*
*Each thought there was one cat too many:*
*So they fought and they fit,*
*And they scratched and they bit,*
*Till, except for their nails*
*And the tips of their tails,*
*Instead of two cats there weren't any.*

(*Traditional*)

**114** *A gaggle of geese,*
*A gangling of goslings,*
*A giggle of girls,*
*A gathering of gossips.*

**115** *King Charles the First to Parliament came,*
*Five good Parliament men to claim;*
*King Charles he had them each by name,*
*Denzyl Holles and Jonathan Pym,*
*And William Strode and after him,*
*Arthur Hazelrigg Esquire*
*And Hampden, Gent, of Buckinghamshire.*

*The man at the gate said "Tickets, please,"*
*Said Charles, "I've come for the five M.P.s."*
*The porter said "Which?" and Charles said*
*  "These:*
*Denzyl Holles and Jonathan Pym,*
*And William Strode and after him,*
*Arthur Hazelrigg Esquire*
*And Hampden, Gent, of Buckinghamshire."*

*In at the great front door he went,*
*The great front door of Parliament,*
*While, out at the back with one consent*
*Went Denzyl Holles and Jonathan Pym,*
*And William Strode and after him,*
*Arthur Hazelrigg Esquire*
*And Hampden, Gent, of Buckinghamshire.*

*Into the street strode Charles the First,*
*His nose was high and his lips were pursed,*
*While, laugh till their rebel sides near burst, did*
*Denzyl Holles and Jonathan Pym,*
*And William Strode and after him,*
*Arthur Hazelrigg Esquire,*
*And Hampden, Gent, of Buckinghamshire.*

*(Hugh Chesterman, "King Charles the First")*

116 *He wouldn't get out and he couldn't get in,*
*The moon man was stuck right on the rim*
*Of his crater.*
*His nose, eyes, one ear*
*On the outside appeared,*
*While from the chin down*
*He was stuck in the ground,*
*And all he could move was his toes*
*Round and round.*
*This man on the moon*
*Like a plug in a balloon*
*Was stuck for quite some time;*
*But then he got thin,*
*And forced out his chin,*
*Then his arms and was so pleased to find,*
*With a bit of a squeeze*
*He could get out his knees,*
*Then he realized his luck,*
*He was no longer stuck!*
*So he scrambled right out*
*And gave a big shout,*
*And he danced on the butter-bright moon.*
(*Fay Hampson,* "*Moon Man*")


117 *Does the man in the moon like music?*
*Does he tootle on his flute or does he croon?*
*Does he slip in something lunar*
*In the way he plays his tune or*
*Does he simply sit and doodle in the moon?*
(*Traditional*)


118 *A tutor who tooted the flute*
*Tried to tutor two tooters to toot,*

Said the two to the tutor,
"Is it easier to toot,
Or to tutor two tooters to toot?"

(*Traditional*)

**119** For a month to dwell
In a dungeon cell;
Growing thin and wizen
In a solitary prison,
Is a poor look-out
For a soldier stout,
Who is longing for the rattle
Of a complicated battle—
For the rum-tum-tum
Of the military drum,
And the guns that go boom! boom!

(*W. S. Gilbert*)

**120** Dreamers, mark the honey bee,
Mark the tree,
Where the blue cap tootletee,
Sings a glee,
Sung to Adam and to Eve,
Here they be!

**121** Cock crows in the morn to tell us to rise,
And he who lies late will never be wise:
For early to bed and early to rise,
Is the way to be healthy, wealthy and wise.

(*Nursery rhyme*)

**122** *The common cormorant or shag,*
*Lays eggs inside a paper bag;*
*The reason you will see no doubt,*
*It is to keep the lightning out.*
*But what that unobservant bird*
*Has never thought of is—a herd*
*Of bears may come with buns,*
*And steal the bags to keep the crumbs.*

*(Edward Lear)*

**123** *Big fleas have little fleas*
*Upon their backs to bite 'em,*
*Little fleas have littler fleas,*
*And so ad infinitum.*

*(After Swift)*

**124** *A complicated gentleman allow me to present,*
*Of all the arts and faculties a terse embodiment:*
*A great arithmetician, who can demonstrate*
*with ease,*
*That two and two are three or five, or anything*
*you please:*
*An eminent logician, who can make it clear to*
*you*
*That black is white—when looked at from the*
*proper point of view:*
*A marvellous philologist, who'll undertake to*
*show*
*That "yes" is but another form of "no."*

*(W. S. Gilbert)*

**125** *A was an apple-pie;*
*B bit it; C cut it;*
*D danced for it; E eyed it;*
*F fought for it; G gaped for it;*
*H hung it up:*
*I inspected it; J jumped for it;*
*K kicked it; L longed for it;*
*M mourned for it; N nodded at it;*
*O opened it;*
*P peeped in it; Q quartered it;*
*R ran for it; S skipped for it;*
*T turned it; U upset it;*
*V viewed it; W wished for it;*
*X Y Z all did the same;*
*And at last the pie was,*
*By final consent,*
*Divided among the whole party.*
                    (*Nursery rhyme*)


**126** *Handy Spandy Jack-a-dandy*
*Loved plum-cake and sugar-candy;*
*He bought some at a grocer's shop*
*And out he came, hip, hap, hop.*
                    (*Nursery rhyme*)


**127** *There was an owl lived in a tree,*
*Wisky, wasky, weedle;*
*And all the words he ever spoke,*
*Were fiddle, faddle, feedle.*
                    (*Nursery rhyme*)

**128** *I had a little nut-tree*
*And nothing would it bear*
*But a silver nutmeg*
*And a golden pear;*
*The king of Spain's daughter*
*Came to visit me,*
*And all for the sake*
*Of my little nut-tree.*
*I skipped over water,*
*I danced over sea,*
*And all the birds of the air*
*Couldn't catch me.*

(*Nursery rhyme*)

**129** *Twenty, nineteen, eighteen,*
*Seventeen, sixteen, fifteen,*
*Fourteen, thirteen, twelve,*
*Eleven, ten, nine,*
*Eight, seven, six,*
*Five, four, three,*
*Two, one.*
*All done!*

(*Nursery rhyme*)

# Nine

# *RANDOM IDEAS*

**130** Animal sounds
>*Bleat like a sheep.*
>*Try some chicken clucks and a cock's crow.*
>*Drone like bees.*
>*Hum on n making it sound like a gnat.*

**131** Mechanical sounds
>*Repeat the word POP making it sound like the exhaust of a motor-boat.*
>*Try a motor-bike approaching and then passing into the distance.*
>*Experiment with train noises and call the destinations of local trains above them.*

**132** Musical sounds
>*Listen to the following instruments and then reproduce them vocally—*
>>*violin*
>>*'cello*
>>*trumpet*
>>*oboe*
>>*drum*
>*Combine a group of instruments and orchestrate a tune for them.*

**133** Move and make sounds

> *Be a gate opening and creak.*
> *Spin like a top and hum.*
> *Become a Martian creature with an appropriate language.*
> *Choose fairy lines from A Midsummer Night's Dream and fly to them;*

Experiment with hums or non-human language. Try the witch scenes from *Macbeth*.

**134** Combine words, phrases, shouts and non-speech sounds to give an impression of—

> *The docks.*
> *Music of the spheres.*
> *A factory starting up early on Monday morning.*
> *A busy street.*
> *An Oriental market.*
> *A telephone exchange.*

Experiment with sound combinations and repeat them rhythmically—

> *woller woller wumbom*
> *bmut din itht*

**135**

| | | |
|---|---|---|
| *dawn chorus* | *esau* | *scornfulness* |
| *football* | *waters* | *befall* |
| *jackdaw* | *fallen* | *enthrall* |
| | *fall* | |
| *scorn* | | *dawn* |
| *falsity* *shore* | | *all* *forbearing* |
| *crawls* | | *shawl* |
| | *talk* | |
| *recall* | *talker* | *forehead* |
| *retort* | *crawling* | *foretold* |
| *enthralling* | *scornful* | *may dawning* |

*This is one stanza from the long poem* Chamber Music *by Bob Cobbing. A group of speakers can use it, each individual working as they wish; from the centre out, across, up and down, or just haphazardly: the overall impression is of the recurring vowel. You could choose other vowels and make your own patterns.*

**136** Choose a mood and list the words occurring in association with it. Choose the best, arrange them in a rhythm sympathetic to the theme and then interpret them.

**137** Keep a look-out for FOUND poems: a flower seed catalogue might yield one; legal forms are worth considering; recipes and instructions offer possibilities.

# Ten

# *VOCAL APPLICATION*

*As well as muscular skill the following passages need concentrated thought and a strong imaginative impulse. They cover a wide range of obvious vocal opportunities.*

**138** *The dawn's precise pronouncement waits*
*With breath of light indrawn,*
*Then forms with smoky, smut-red lips*
*The great O of the sun.*

> *(Laurie Lee, "The Edge of Day")*

**139** *A wind sways the pines,*
*And below*
*Not a breath of wild air;*
*Still as the mosses that glow*
*On the flooring and over the lines*
*Of the roots here and there.*
*The pine-tree drops its dead;*
*They are quiet, as under the sea.*
*Overhead, overhead*
*Rushes life in a race,*
*As the clouds the clouds chase;*
*And we go,*
*And we drop like the fruits of the tree,*
*Even we,*

*Even so.*

(*George Meredith, "Dirge in Words"*)

**140** *Oh ye! who have your eye-balls vex'd and tired,*
*Feast them upon the wideness of the Sea;*
*Oh ye! whose ears are dinn'd with uproar rude,*
*Sit ye near some old cavern's mouth, and brood*
*Until ye start, as if the sea-nymphs quired!*

(*Keats, "Sonnet"*)

**141** *I cannot see what flowers are at my feet,*
*Nor what soft incense hangs upon the boughs,*
*But, in embalmèd darkness, guess each sweet*
*Wherewith the seasonable month endows*
*The grass, the thicket, and the fruit-tree wild;*
*White hawthorn, and the pastoral eglantine;*
*Fast-fading violets cover'd up in leaves;*
*A mid-May's eldest child,*
*The coming musk-rose, full of dewy wine,*
*The murmurous haunt of flies on summer eves.*

(*Keats, "Ode to a Nightingale"*)

**142** *Remember now thy Creator in the days of thy*
*youth, while the evil days come not, nor the years*
*draw nigh, when thou shalt say, I have no*
*pleasure in them;*

*While the sun, or the light, or the moon, or*
*the stars, be not darkened, nor the clouds return*
*after the rain:*

*In the day when the keepers of the house shall*
*tremble, and the strong men shall bow them-*
*selves, and the grinders cease because they are*
*few, and those that look out of the windows be*
*darkened.*

*And the doors shall be shut in the street, when the sound of the grinding is low, and he shall rise up at the voice of a bird, and all the daughters of music shall be brought low;*

*Also when they shall be afraid of that which is high, and fears shall be in the way, and the almond tree shall flourish, and the grasshopper shall be a burden, and desire shall fail: because man goeth to his long home, and the mourners go about the streets.*

*Or ever the silver cord be loosed, or the golden bowl be broken, or the pitcher be broken at the fountain, or the wheel broken at the cistern.*

*Then shall the dust return to the earth as it was: and the spirit shall return unto God who gave it.*

*(Ecclesiastes)*

**143** *These have I loved:*
*White plates and cups, clean-gleaming,*
*Ringed with blue lines; and feathery, faery dust;*
*Wet roofs, beneath the lamp-light; the strong crust*
*Of friendly bread; and many tasting food;*
*Rainbows; and the blue bitter smoke of wood;*
*Then, the cool kindliness of sheets, that soon*
*Smooth away trouble; and the rough male kiss*
*Of blankets; grainy wood; live hair that is*
*Shining and free; blue-massing clouds; the keen*
*Unpassioned beauty of a great machine;*
*The benison of hot water; furs to touch;*
*The good smell of old clothes; and others such—*
*The comfortable smell of friendly fingers.*

*Hair's fragrance, and the musty reek that lingers*
*About dead leaves and last year's ferns . . .*

(*Rupert Brooke, "The Great Lover"*)

**144** Miss Bates came in talking and had not finished her speech under many minutes after her being admitted into the circle at the fire. As the door opened she was heard,

"So very obliging of you!—No rain at all. Nothing to signify. I do not care for myself. Quite thick shoes. And Jane declares—Well!—Well! This is brilliant indeed!—This is admirable!—Excellently contrived, upon my word. Nothing wanting. Could not have imagined it —So well lighted up. Jane, Jane, look—did you ever see anything? Ah! dear Mrs. Elton, so obliged to you for the carriage!—excellent time.—Jane and I quite ready. Did not keep the horses a moment. Most comfortable carriage. Thank you, my mother is remarkably well. Gone to Mr. Woodhouse's. Dear Miss Woodhouse, how do you do?—Very well, I thank you, quite well. Upon my word, Miss Woodhouse, you do look—how do you like Jane's hair? No hairdresser from London I think could—Ah! Dr. Hughes, I declare—and Mrs. Hughes. Mrs. Otway, I protest! Such a host of friends!—And such a noble fire!—I am quite roasted. No coffee, I thank you, for me— never take coffee.—A little tea if you please, sir, by and by,—no hurry.—Oh! here it comes. Everything so good!"

(*Jane Austen, "Emma"*)

**145** *Cloud-puffball, torn tufts, tossed pillows flaunt*
  *forth, then chevy on an air-*
*built thoroughfare: heaven-roysterers, in gay-*
  *gangs they throng; they glitter in marches.*
*Down roughcast, down dazzling whitewash,*
  *wherever an elm arches,*
*Shivelights and shadowtackle in long lashes lace,*
  *lance, and pair.*

(*Gerard Manley Hopkins, "That Nature*
*is a Heraclitean Fire"*)

**146** 1872 AUGUST 10th. I was looking at high
waves. The breakers always are parallel to the
coast and shape themselves to it except where
the curve is sharp however the wind blows.
They are rolled out by the shallowing shore
just as a piece of putty between the palms
whatever its shape runs into a long roll. The
slant ruck or crease one sees in them shows the
way of the wind. The regularity of the barrels
surprised and charmed the eye; the edge behind the comb or crest was as smooth and
bright as glass. It may be noticed to be green
behind and silver white in front: the silver
marks where the air begins, the pure white is
foam, the green, solid water. Then looked at to
the right or left they are scrolled over like
mouldboards or feathers or jibsails seen by the
edge. It is pretty to see the hollow of the
barrel disappearing as the white comb on each
side runs along the wave gaining ground till the
two meet at a pitch and crush and overlap
each other.

(*Gerard Manley Hopkins, "Journal"*)

**147** *O wild West Wind, thou breath of Autumn's*
*being*
*Thou from whose unseen presence the leaves*
*dead*
*Are driven like ghosts from an enchanter fleeing,*

*Yellow, and black, and pale, and hectic red,*
*Pestilence-stricken multitudes! O thou*
*Who chariotest to their dark wintry bed*

*The wingèd seeds, where they lie cold and low,*
*Each like a corpse within its grave, until*
*Thine azure sister of the Spring shall blow*

*Her clarion o'er the dreaming earth, and fill*
*(Driving sweet buds like flocks to feed in air)*
*With living hues and odours plain and hill;*

*Wild Spirit, which art moving everywhere;*
*Destroyer and preserver; hear, O, hear!*
  *(Shelley, "Ode to the West Wind")*

**148** *And the sun went down, and the stars came out*
*far over the summer sea,*
*But never a moment ceased the fight of the one*
*and the fifty-three.*
*Ship after ship, the whole night long, their high-*
*built galleons came,*
*Ship after ship, the whole night long, with her*
*battle-thunder and flame;*
*Ship after ship, the whole night long, drew back*
*with her dead and her shame.*
*For some were sunk, and many were shatter'd,*
*and so could fight us no more—*

*God of battles, was ever a battle like this in the world before?*

(*Tennyson, "The Revenge"*)

**149** *O Clap your hands, all ye people; shout unto God with voice of triumph.*

*God is gone up with a shout, the Lord with the sound of a trumpet.*

*Sing praises unto God, sing praises: sing praises unto our King, sing praises.*

*For God is the king of all the earth.*

(*Psalm 47*)

# Eleven

# PRACTICE PASSAGES

*These are all advanced passages and cover a wide range of vocal demands. They begin with* Formal Language, *pass through* Formal-Colloquial *and* Colloquial *to* Informal Colloquial.

**150**                    *Virtue*

*Sweet day, so cool, so calm, so bright,*
*The bridal of the earth and sky:*
*The dew shall weep thy fall tonight;*
  *For thou must die.*

*Sweet rose, whose hue angry and brave*
*Bids the rash gazer wipe his eye:*
*Thy root is ever in its grave,*
  *And thou must die.*

*Sweet spring, full of sweet days and roses,*
*A box where sweets compacted lie;*
*My music shows ye have your closes,*
  *And all must die.*

*Only a sweet and virtuous soul,*
*Like season'd timber, never gives;*
*But though the whole world turn to coal,*
  *Then chiefly lives.*

          *(George Herbert, ''Virtue'')*

**151**                    *Psalms 148 and 150*

(*Group speaking*)

*Praise ye the Lord. Praise ye the Lord from the heavens: praise him in the heights.*

*Praise ye him, all his angels: praise ye him, all his hosts.*

*Praise ye him, sun and moon: praise him, all ye stars of light.*

*Praise him, ye heaven of heavens, and ye waters that be above the heavens.*

*Let them praise the name of the Lord: for he commanded, and they were created.*

*Praise the Lord from the earth, ye dragons and all deeps:*

*Fire, and hail: snow, and vapour; stormy wind fulfilling his word:*

*Mountains, and all hills; fruitful trees, and all cedars:*

*Beasts, and all cattle; creeping things, and flying fowl:*

*Kings of the earth, and all people: princes, and all judges of the earth:*

*Both young men, and maidens; old men, and children:*

*Let them praise the name of the Lord: for his name alone is excellent; his glory is above the earth and heaven.*

*Praise ye the Lord. Praise God in his sanctuary: praise him in the firmament of his power.*

*Praise him for his mighty acts: praise him according to his excellent greatness.*

*Praise him with the sound of the trumpet; praise him with the psaltery and harp.*

*Praise him with the timbrel and dance, praise him with the stringed instruments and organs.*

*Praise him upon the loud cymbals: praise him upon the high sounding cymbals.*

*Let everything that hath breath praise the Lord. Praise ye the Lord.*

**152**          *Spelt from Sibyl's Leaves*

*Earnest, earthless, equal, attuneable, vaulty, voluminous, . . . stupendous*

*Evening strains to be time's vast, womb-of-all, home-of-all, hearse-of-all night.*

*Her fond yellow hornlight wound to the west, her wild hollow hoarlight hung to the height*

*Waste; her earliest stars, earl-stars, stars principal, overbend us,*

*Fire-featuring heaven. For earth her being has unbound, her dapple is at an end, as-*

*tray or aswarm, all throughther, in throngs; self in self steeped and pashed—quite*

*Disremembering, dismembering all now. Heart, you round me right*

*With: Our evening is over us; our night whelms, whelms, and will end us.*

*Only the beak-leaved boughs dragonish damask the tool-smooth bleak light; black,*

*Ever so black on it. Our tale, O our oracle! Let life, waned, ah let life wind*

*Off her once skeined stained veined variety upon, all on two spools; part, pen, pack*

*Now her all in two flocks, two folds—black, white; right, wrong; reckon but, mind*

*But these two; ware of a world where but these two tell, each off the other; of a rack*

*Where, selfwrung, selfstrung, sheathe—and*
*shelterless, thoughts against thoughts in*
*groans grind.*

(*Gerard Manley Hopkins, "Spelt from*
*Sibyl's Leaves"*)

**153** *RUMOUR: Open your ears; for which of you*
*will stop*
*The vent of hearing when loud Rumour speaks?*
*I, from the Orient, to the drooping West*
*(Making the wind my post-horse) still unfold*
*The acts commenced on this ball of earth.*
*Upon my tongues, continual slanders ride,*
*The which, in every language, I pronounce,*
*Stuffing the ears of men with false reports:*
*I speak of peace, while covert enmity*
*(Under the smile of safety) wounds the world:*
*And who but Rumour, who but only I*
*Make fearful musters, and prepar'd defence,*
*Whiles the big year, swollen with some other*
*griefs,*
*Is thought with child, by the stern tyrant, War,*
*And no such matter? Rumour is a pipe*
*Blown by surmises, jealousies, conjectures;*
*And of so easy and so plain a stop,*
*That the blunt monster, with uncounted heads,*
*The still-discordant, wavering multitude,*
*Can play upon it. But what need I thus*
*My well-known body to anatomize*
*Among my household? Why is Rumour here?*
*I run before King Harry's victory,*
*Who in a bloody field by Shrewsbury*
*Hath beaten down young Hotspur and his*
*troops,*

*Quenching the flame of bold rebellion,*
*Even with the rebels' blood. But what mean I*
*To speak so true at first? My office is*
*To noise abroad that Harry Monmouth fell*
*Under the wrath of noble Hotspur's sword:*
*And that the King, before the Douglas' rage*
*Stoop'd his anointed head, as low as death.*
*This have I rumour'd through the peasant towns,*
*Between that royal field of Shrewsbury,*
*And this worm-eaten hold of ragged stone*
*Where Hotspur's father, old Northumberland,*
*Lies crafty-sick. The posts come tiring on,*
*And not a man of them brings other news*
*Than they have learn'd of me. From Rumour's*
*tongues,*
*They bring smooth comforts false, worse than*
*true wrongs.*

(*Shakespeare, Henry IV (Part II), Introduction*)


**154**    *Trio for Two Cats and a Trombone*
              (*Group of three voices*)

*Long steel grass—*
*The white soldiers pass—*
*The light is braying like an ass.*
*See*
*The tall Spanish jade*
*With hair black as nightshade*
*Worn as a cockade!*
*Flee*
*Her eyes' gasconade*
*And her gown's parade*
(*As stiff as a brigade*).
*Tee-hee!*

*The hard and braying light*
*Is zebra'd black and white*
*It will take away the slight*
*And free*
*Tinge of the mouth-organ sound,*
*(Oyster-stall notes) oozing round*
*Her flounces as they sweep the ground.*
*The*
*Trumpet and the drum*
*And the martial cornet come*
*To make the people dumb—*
*But we*
*Won't wait for sly-foot night*
*(Moonlight, watered milk-white, bright)*
*To make clear the declaration*
*Of our Paphian vocation,*
*Beside the castanetted sea,*
*Where stalks Il Capitaneo*
*Swaggart braggadocio*
*Sword and moustachio—*
*He*
*Is green as a cassada*
*And his hair is an armada.*
*To the jade "Come kiss me harder"*
*He called across the battlements as she*
*Heard our voices thin and shrill*
*As the steely grasses' thrill*
*Or the sound of the onycha*
*When the phoca has the pica*
*In the palace of the Queen Chinee!*

(*Edith Sitwell*)

**155**                    *Music on the Moon*

*The pianos on the moon are so long*
*The pianists' hand must be fifteen fingers strong.*

*The violins on the moon are so violent*
*They have to be sunk in deep wells, and then they*
    *only seem to be silent.*

*The bassoons on the moon blow no notes*
*But huge blue loons that flap slowly away with*
    *undulating throats.*

*Now harmonies on the moon are humorous,*
*The tunes produce German Measles, but the*
    *speckles are more numerous.*

*Of a trumpet on the moon you can never hear*
    *enough*
*Because it puffs the trumpeter up like a balloon*
    *and he floats off.*

*Double basses on the moon are a risk all right,*
*At the first note enormous black hands appear*
    *and carry off everything in sight.*

*Even a triangle on the moon is risky,*
*One ping—and there's your head a half bottle*
    *of Irish whisky.*

*In the same way, be careful with the flute—*
*Because wherever he is, your father will find*
    *himself converted into a disgusting old boot.*

*On the whole it's best to stick to the moon's drums,*
*Whatever damage they do is so far off in space the news never comes.*

(*Ted Hughes, "The Earth-Owl and Other Moon People"*)

**156** *The Horses*

*I climbed through the woods in the hour-before-dawn dark.*
*Evil air, a frost-making stillness,*

*Not a leaf, not a bird,—*
*A world cast in frost. I came out above the wood*

*Where my breath left tortuous statues in the iron light.*
*But the valleys were draining the darkness*

*Till the moorline—blackening dregs of the brightening grey—*
*Halved the sky ahead. And I saw the horses:*

*Huge in the dense grey—ten together—*
*Megalith still. They breathed, making no move,*

*With draped manes and tilted hind-hoves,*
*Making no sound.*

*I passed: not one snorted or jerked its head.*
*Grey silent fragments*

*Of a grey silent world.*

*I listened in emptiness on the moor-ridge.*
*The curlew's tear turned its edge on the silence.*

*Slowly detail leafed from the darkness. Then the sun*
*Orange, red, red erupted*

*Silently, and splitting to its core tore and flung cloud,*
*Shook the gulf open, showed blue,*

*And the big planets hanging—*
*I turned*

*Stumbling in the fever of a dream, down towards*
*The dark woods, from the kindling tops,*

*And came to the horses.*
                    *There, still they stood,*
*But now steaming and glistening under the flow of light,*

*Their draped stone manes, their tilted hind-hooves*
*Stirring under a thaw while all around them*

*The frost showed its fires. But still they made no sound.*
*Not one snorted or stamped,*

*Their hung heads patient as the horizons,*
*High over the valleys, in the red levelling rays—*

*In din of the crowded streets, going among the years, the faces,*
*May I still meet my memory in so lonely a place*

*Between the streams and the red clouds, hearing curlews,*
*Hearing the horizons endure.*

                    *(Ted Hughes, "The Horses")*

I was set down from the carrier's cart at the age of three; and there with a sense of bewilderment and terror my life in the village began.

The June grass, amongst which I stood, was taller than I was, and I wept. I had never been so close to grass before. It towered above me and all around me, each blade tattooed with tiger-skins of sunlight. It was knife-edged, dark, and a wicked green, thick as a forest and alive with grasshoppers that chirped and chattered and leapt through the air like monkeys.

I was lost and didn't know where to move. A tropic heat oozed up from the ground, rank with sharp odours of roots and nettles. Snow-clouds of elder-blossom banked in the sky, showering upon me the fumes and flakes of their sweet and giddy suffocation. High overhead ran frenzied larks, screaming, as though the sky were tearing apart.

For the first time in my life I was out of sight of humans. For the first time in my life I was alone in a world whose behaviour I could neither predict nor fathom: a world of birds that squealed, of plants that stank, of insects that sprang about without warning. I was lost and I did not expect to be found again. I put back my head and howled, and the sun hit me smartly on the face, like a bully.

From this daylight nightmare I was awakened, as from many another, by the appearance of my sisters. They came scrambling and calling up the steep rough bank, and parting the long grass found me. Faces of rose, familiar, living; huge shining faces hung up like shields between me and the sky; faces with grins and white teeth (some broken) to be conjured up like genii with a howl, brushing off terror with their broad scoldings and affection. They leaned over me—one, two, three— their mouths smeared with red currants and their hands dripping with juice.

"There, there, it's all right, don't you wail any more. Come down 'ome and we'll stuff you with currants."

And Marjorie, the eldest, lifted me into her long brown hair, and ran me jogging down the path and through the steep rose-filled garden, and set me down on the cottage doorstep, which was our home, though I couldn't believe it.

That was the day we came to the village, in the summer of the last year of the First World War. To a cottage that stood in a half-acre of garden on a steep bank above a lake; a cottage with three floors and a cellar and a treasure in the walls, with a pump and apple trees, syringa and strawberries, rooks in the chimneys, frogs in the cellar, mushrooms on the ceiling, and all for three and sixpence a week.

(*Laurie Lee*)

**158**     *Three Sundays and a Summary*

*Platform Sunday*
*Someone whistles a casual hymn*
*As the train edges out,*

*Slicing the sun.*
*An afterthought*
*Among the black and white*
*'Observers' and the 'Mirrors'*
*Littered over the prickly seats,*
*And hot confusion*
*Of empty beer cans*
*In the buffet,*
*While sleepers*
*Nod reverent heads*
*In the first class,*
*And snore*
*Into the long*
*Sermon of wheels.*

*High Sunday (also Happened to be Remembrance Sunday)*

*This morning*
*A drunken sinner,*
*Clutching the coffee cup*
*With pastry fingers mesmerized,*
*With rolling pin head*
*That nods over a red flower*
*With gin and lime sympathy.*
*Nothing disturbs me.*
*Not even silence. (silence)*

*Sober Sunday*

*The bells howl*
*Church.*
*Padding, frozen,*
*To clutch the little rail*
*At the top.*

*Scared for some reason.*
*The paper flesh*
*Sticks in my throat*
*Like a fishbone,*
*It won't get down*
*In time for the blood—*
*Wait—*
*But they don't*
*It's all so rhythmical,*
*The collar frowns,*
*His gold clinks the cup—*
*Panic—*
*They are chasing me*
*Helter skelter,*
*Down the aisle.*

*Summary*

*All this time,*
*Caught in one*
*Frenzied hymn,*
*No shape, no place,*
*You cannot place*
*Your finger on*
*One note,*
*It is impossible*
*To sing.*

(*Liz Holmes, "Three Sundays*
　　　　*and a Summary"*)

**159**　　　　*From Three Men in a Boat*

Harris asked me if I'd ever been in the maze at
Hampton Court. He said he went in once to
show somebody else the way. He had studied

it on a map, and it was so simple that it seemed foolish—hardly worth the twopence charged for admission. Harris said he thought that map must have been got up as a practical joke, because it wasn't a bit like the real thing, and only misleading. It was a country cousin that Harris took in. He said:

"We'll just go in here, so that you can say you've been, but it's very simple. It's absurd to call it a maze. You keep on taking the first turning to the right. We'll just walk round for ten minutes, and then go and get some lunch."

They met some people soon after they had got inside, who said they had been there for three-quarters of an hour, and had had about enough of it. Harris told them they could follow him if they liked; he was just going in, and then should turn round and come out again. They said it was very kind of him, and fell behind, and followed.

They picked up various other people who wanted to get it over, as they went along, until they had absorbed all the persons in the maze. People who had given up all hopes of getting either in or out, or of ever seeing their home and friends again, plucked up courage, at the sight of Harris and his party, and joined the procession, blessing him. Harris said he should judge there must have been twenty people following him, in all; and one woman with a baby, who had been there all the morning, insisted on taking his arm, for fear of losing him.

Harris kept on turning to the right, but it

seemed a long way, and his cousin said he supposed it was a very big maze.

"Oh, one of the largest in Europe," said Harris.

"Yes, it must be," replied his cousin, "because we've walked a good two miles already."

Harris began to think it rather strange himself, but he held on until, at last, they passed the half of a penny bun on the ground that Harris's cousin swore he had noticed there seven minutes ago. Harris said: "Oh, impossible!" but the woman with the baby said, "Not at all," as she herself had taken it from the child, and thrown it down there, just before she met Harris. She also added that she wished she never had met Harris, and expressed an opinion that he was an imposter. That made Harris mad, and he produced his map, and explained his theory.

"The map may be all right enough," said one of the party, "if you know whereabouts in it we are now."

Harris didn't know, and suggested the best thing to do would be to go back to the entrance, and begin again. For the beginning again part of it there was not much enthusiasm; but with regard to the advisability of going back to the entrance there was complete unanimity, and so they turned, and trailed after Harris again, in the opposite direction. About ten minutes more passed, and then they found themselves in the centre.

Harris thought at first of pretending that

that was what he had been aiming at; but the crowd looked dangerous, and he decided to treat is as an accident.

Anyhow, they had got something to start from then. They did now know where they were, and the map was once more consulted, and the thing seemed simpler than ever, and off they started for the third time.

And three minutes later they were back in the centre again.

After that they simply couldn't get anywhere else. Whatever way they turned brought them back to the middle. It became so regular at length that some people stopped there, and waited for the others to take a walk round, and come back to them. Harris drew out his map again, but the sight of it only infuriated the mob, and they told him to go and curl his hair with it. Harris said that he couldn't help feeling that, to a certain extent, he had become unpopular.

They all got crazy at last, and sang out for the keeper, and the man came and climbed up the ladder outside, and shouted out directions to them. But all their heads were, by this time, in such a confused whirl that they were incapable of grasping anything, and so the man told them to stop where they were, and he would come to them. They huddled together, and waited; and he climbed down, and came in.

He was a young keeper, as luck would have it, and new to the business; and when he got in, he couldn't get to them, and then *he* got lost.

They caught sight of him, every now and then, rushing about on the other side of the hedge, and he would see them, and they would wait there for about five minutes, and then he would reappear again in exactly the same spot, and ask them where they had been.

They had to wait until one of the old keepers came back from his dinner before they got out.

Harris said he thought it was a very fine maze, so far as he was a judge; and we agreed that we would try to get George to go into it, on our way back.

(*Jerome K. Jerome*, "*Three Men in a Boat*")

**160** *Be Good, Sweet Maid*

BRENDA. This boy at the factory, it's like . . . magic. You think of him, and he thinks of you: he has to. You want him to do something, pick up your india rubber, or take you to the pictures, and he does it. Like magic. It makes you feel . . . powerful. I think I'd have made a good witch. All this time I've gone on letting things happen to me. Now they're going to happen to other people. Because I want them to. I'm all cold and hard and tight inside myself and ever so clever. All the silliness is over and I know what I've got. This boy at the office, he's just an experiment, like as if I was sitting over a bubbling cauldron and putting pieces of him into it.

(*C. E. Webber*, "*Be Good, Sweet Maid*")

c/o The Opera House
Cork, Ireland

So you've been wondering where I've landed up have you! Well in all truth I've many times thought of writing then dispensed with the idea—when it's all down on paper whatever one's doing sounds pretty trivial and boring to someone else. Of course I'm not in the least bit bored, and think it's the best thing alive to be practically living in the Opera House, and in its own Irish way this is an excellent start, far from the Metropolis, where one can settle down and do bad things interspersed with good things, and know that it's not likely to affect the future. A six-week season is what I'm embarked on—half way through now—so I return about mid-October, to the vistas of unemployment and my agent's office. Some super parts have come my way while I've been here, and I've learnt an enormous amount already—doing comedy all the time, but a change next week, which I'm looking forward to immensely. I'm fine then except right now I'm a bit hungry—my landlady doesn't run to lunch on Sunday, but I guess I'll survive till six.

Ireland is so old fashioned in many ways you know—people generally are not very smart—old ladies everywhere wrapped up in enormous black blankets, stray dogs, everyone madly crossing themselves on buses each time they pass a R.C. church—endless horse-drawn carts with decrepit-looking men carting rubbish about or selling things, and on Saturday I had a few hours and went to Youghal—a seaside place, very quiet—with whitewashed walls, almost like the South of France in places. Then on to Whiting Bay—completely deserted, just a little man with horse and cart collecting stones. They farm right up to the sea practically . . . that bit was very Irish. Now I'm really going to stop.